# I'm good at

# Maths

## Eileen Day

**www.raintreepublishers.co.uk**
Visit our website to find out more information about **Raintree** books.

To order:
☎ Phone 44 (0) 1865 888112
▤ Send a fax to 44 (0) 1865 314091
💻 Visit the Heinemann Bookshop at **www.raintreepublishers.co.uk** to browse our catalogue and order online.

First published in Great Britain by Raintree, Halley Court, Jordan Hill, Oxford OX2 8EJ, part of Harcourt Education.
Raintree is a registered trademark of Harcourt Education Ltd.

Editorial: Nick Hunter and Diyan Leake
Design: Michelle Lisseter
Picture Research: Alan Gottlieb and Amor Montes de Oca
Production: Lorraine Hicks

Originated by Dot Gradations
Printed and bound in China by South China Printing Company

ISBN 1 844 21505 9
07 06 05 04 03
10 9 8 7 6 5 4 3 2 1

**British Library Cataloguing in Publication Data**
Day, Eileen
Maths. – (I'm good at)
510
A full catalogue record for this book is available from the British Library.

**Acknowledgements**
The publishers would like to thank the following for permission to reproduce photographs: Bob Daemmrich Photography, Inc., **21**; Corbis/Jose Luis Pelaez, Inc., **16**; Getty Images/Stone, **18**; Heinemann Library/Robert Lifson, **5**, **6**, **7**, **8**, **9**, **10**, **11**, **12**, **14**, **15**, **17**, **19**, **22**, **23**, **24**; Johnathan Banks/Rex Features, **4**; Photo Researchers, Inc./Russell D. Curtis, **13**; Stock Boston/Bob Daemmrich, **20**.

Cover photograph reproduced with permission of Corbis/Tom & Dee Ann McCarthy.

Every effort has been made to contact copyright holders of any material reproduced in this book. Any omissions will be rectified in subsequent printings if notice is given to the publishers.

Some words are shown in bold, **like this**.
They are explained in the glossary on page 23.

# Contents

# What is maths?

Maths is using numbers and symbols.

Some numbers tell you how much things cost.

Other numbers tell you where someone lives.

You can use maths every day.

# What is counting?

Counting is finding out how many.

You can put things together to count them.

You can count the days of the week on a **calendar**.

There are seven days in a week.

# What is sorting?

**Sorting** is putting things in groups.

You can sort all kinds of things.

You can sort fruit at home.

You can sort apples by colour.

# What is a pattern?

A pattern is seeing the same thing again and again.

Can you see the pattern in this line?

You can make a pattern when you string beads.

You can string red beads, then blue.

# What is a shape?

A shape is how something looks.

Everything has a shape.

You can draw a shape.

You can make a heart for your Mum.

# What is a pair?

A pair is two things that match.

Your feet are a pair.

You can make pairs with socks.

You can put matching socks together.

# What is telling time?

hand

Telling time is reading numbers on a clock.

The **hands** show the time.

The hands on this clock show
8 o'clock.

Time to leave for school!

# What is measuring?

When you measure, you find out how big something is.

You can measure with a **ruler**.

You can measure with shapes.

This barn is nine bears long!

# How do I feel when I do maths?

You feel proud when you do maths.

It makes you feel special.

Doing maths makes you
feel important.

When you do maths, you can help
other people.

# Quiz

What will show how tall you are?

Look for the answer on page 24.

# Glossary

**calendar**
list or table that shows the days, weeks and months of a year

**hands**
parts of the clock that go around and point to the numbers so we can tell the time

**ruler**
wooden or plastic stick with marks used to measure how long something is

**sorting**
dividing things into groups

# Index

Answer to quiz on page 22

A ruler can show how tall you are.

# Titles in the I'm Good At series include:

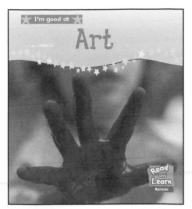

Hardback       1 844 21503 2

Hardback       1 844 21500 8

Hardback       1 844 21501 6

Hardback       1 844 21502 4

Hardback       1 844 21505 9

Hardback       1 844 21504 0

Find out about the other titles in this series on our website www.raintreepublishers.co.uk

# DISCOVER THROUGH CRAFT

# THE CELTS AND THE IRON AGE

By Jen Green

W

Franklin Watts
This edition published in 2016 by The Watts Publishing Group

Copyright © The Watts Publishing Group 2015
All rights reserved.

Series editor: Amy Stephenson
Series designer: Jeni Child
Crafts: Rita Storey
Craft photography: Tudor Photography
Picture researcher: Diana Morris

Picture credits:
The Art Archive/Alamy: 24b. Anton Balazh/Shutterstock: 6t. Caroline Lena
Becker/CC. Wikimedia: 7b. Cammerraydave/Dreamstime: 18-19 bg. CeStu/CC
Wikimedia: 32. Claire/Colrain Seed Farm: 14cl. David Crosbie1/Dreamstime: 31.
Mark Davidson/Alamy: 12t. De Agostini/SuperStock: 19t. CM Dixon/HIP Topfoto:
18r. Ealdgyth/CC Wikimedia: 6b, 20b. Mary Evans PL: 15t, 16t, 22t. Shaun
Finch/Alamy: 19b. Werner Forman Archive: 22b. Fottoo/Dreamstime: 26t.
Fuzzypeg/CC Wikimedia: 5t. Joe Gough/Dreamstime: 11bl. Jaroslaw Grudzinski/
Shutterstock: 24t. Gt Media/Dreamstime: 10br. Jorg Hackemann/Dreamstime:
14bl. Hannah6d/Dreamstime: 30. Hemis/Alamy: 8b. IgOrzh Dreamstime:
22-23bg. Johnbod/CC Wikimedia: 5b. Ian Keirle/Dreamstime: 10bl, 24c. Last
Refuge/Robert Harding: 28b. Lilkar/Dreamstime: 14br. David Lyons/Alamy:
front cover c. Mantonature/istockphoto: 12b. Mirceaux Dreamstime: 14bc.
Mschmeling/Dreamstime: 4t. Christian Musat/Dreamstime: 14c. Museum of
London: 15b, 18l. © Museums of Scotland: 11r. © National Museum of Wales:
8t. Naturablichter/Dreamstime: 23c. nbiebach/Shutterstock: 10-11bg. paintings/
Shutterstock: 14cr. photocell/Shutterstock: 6-7 bg. Ramen: 16c, 16b. Rosemania/
CC Wikimedia: 20t. Alfio Scisetti/Shutterstock: 14-15 bg. Shutterball/Dreamstime:
23t. Skyscan Photolibrary/Alamy: 1, 10t. St Albans District Council/PAS Attribution-
ShareAlike License: 20c. stocker1970/Shutterstock: 27t. SusaZoom/Shutterstock:
26-27 bg. Titanchik/Dreamstime: 7t. Claudio Vizia/Dreamstime: 26b. Wikimedia
Commons: 28t. Witoldkr1/Dreamstime: 23tr.

Every attempt has been made to clear copyright.
Should there be any inadvertent omission please apply
to the publisher for rectification.

Dewey number: 936.4
ISBN: 978 1 4451 3749 0

Printed in China.

Franklin Watts
An imprint of
Hachette Children's Group
Part of The Watts Publishing Group
Carmelite House
50 Victoria Embankment
London EC4Y 0DZ

An Hachette UK Company
www.hachette.co.uk

www.franklinwatts.co.uk

# CONTENTS

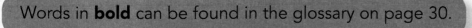

Words in **bold** can be found in the glossary on page 30.

Some of the projects in this book require scissors, paint, glue, garden wire and a kitchen knife. One project also requires the use of an oven. We would recommend that children are supervised by an adult when using these things.

# WHO WERE THE CELTS?

The Celts were an **ancient** people who lived in Europe about 2,700 years ago. They lived during the **Iron Age**, which began about 2,800 years ago.

A map of the area the Celts lived in 2,500 years ago.

## Raiders and traders

Celtic **culture** began in what is now Austria about 2,700 years ago. Around 200 years later (2,500 years ago) it had spread through Europe to Britain and Ireland. The Celts were not an empire like the Roman Empire. But Celts in different areas did speak similar languages and shared a common culture. Experts believe that Celts first came to Britain and Ireland as traders and raiders and many decided to stay.

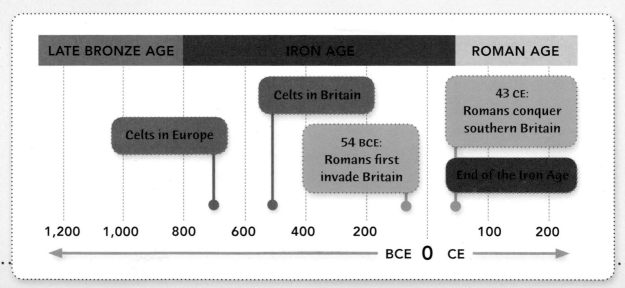

| LATE BRONZE AGE | IRON AGE | ROMAN AGE |
| --- | --- | --- |

Celts in Britain

Celts in Europe

54 BCE: Romans first invade Britain

43 CE: Romans conquer southern Britain

End of the Iron Age

1,200   1,000   800   600   400   200        100   200

BCE **0** CE

4

## Age of iron

The Celts were brave warriors. They were also farmers, traders and skilled craftspeople, who made beautiful and useful objects from metal, stone and pottery. **Bronze** was used to make many objects, but iron was the main metal used to make tools and weapons. Celtic rule in Britain came to an end when the Celts were defeated by the Romans in 43 CE. This date also marks the end of Britain's Iron Age.

## How do we know?

The Celts did not write down their own history. We know about them through Greek and Roman writers. These writers described the Celts as a brave people who loved eating, drinking, horses and fighting. We also know about the Celts from objects, including jewellery and weapons and from the **remains** of their **hill forts** and houses. Experts called **archaeologists** study these remains to find out about Celtic life.

## Quick FACTS

- Celtic culture began in Europe and spread to Britain and Ireland.
- The Celts lived during the Iron Age.
- Iron was the main metal used to make tools and weapons and the Celts were skilled craftspeople.
- The Celts were defeated by the Romans.

This beautiful mirror (top) and decorated shield (above) are both made from bronze.

### QUIZ TIME!

What was the time before the Iron Age called?

a. the Bronze Age
b. the Silver Age
c. the Gold Age

Answer on page 32.

# CELTIC SOCIETY

The Celts lived in large groups called **tribes** that were ruled by a king or queen. Tribes were split into smaller, family **clans**. Each clan was ruled by a **chieftain**, who led warriors into battle.

## Four groups

Experts believe Celtic society was divided into four main groups: nobles, freemen, labourers and slaves. The chieftain, king or queen came from a noble family. As well as being a warrior, he or she owned land and many cattle. Other noblemen were warriors too, but they could also be priests (druids), poets (bards) or master craftsmen.

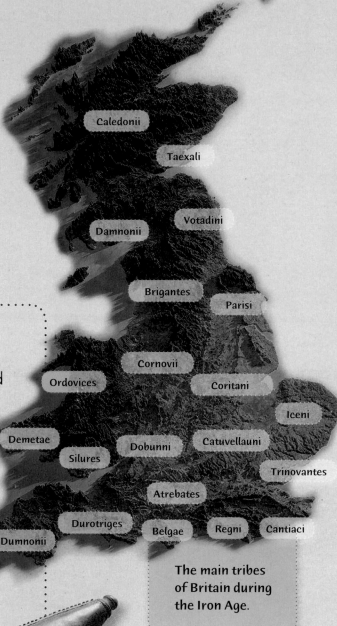

Caledonii
Taexali
Votadini
Damnonii
Brigantes
Parisi
Cornovii
Ordovices
Coritani
Iceni
Demetae
Dobunni
Catuvellauni
Silures
Trinovantes
Atrebates
Durotriges
Belgae
Regni
Cantiaci
Dumnonii

The main tribes of Britain during the Iron Age.

This Celtic chieftain's helmet is made from bronze.

**QUIZ TIME!**

Which is the name of a Celtic tribe from Ireland?

a. **Dan**

b. **Daring**

c. **Darini**

Answer on page 32.

## Druids and bards

Druids and bards were men of learning. As well as being religious leaders, druids also acted as judges. They gave advice to the chieftain, who might send them to make peace with a rival tribe. Women could be druidesses. Bards were official poets who made up poems and songs about the clan's victories in battle.

A **blacksmith** hammers a piece of metal into shape on an anvil. Blacksmiths today use similar tools to blacksmiths in the Iron Age.

## Freemen

Below the nobles were freemen, who were mostly farmers. Like nobles they could own land, or **rent** it from the chieftain. Some freemen were skilled craftsmen, such as blacksmiths.

This stone statue of a Celtic bard was found in France.

### HAVE A GO

Who's in your tribe? Think about all the people you know: family, friends, classmates at school and teachers. You could also include other people you come into contact with, such as shopkeepers or your doctor. Draw a diagram of your tribe with your clan (family) in the centre.

**?** What jobs do you think the slaves did? Turn the page to find out.

## Labourers and slaves

The lower classes were not free. They worked as farm labourers, servants or miners. Lowest of the low were slaves who had been captured in battle. They did the worst jobs, such as cleaning out stables, and were put in chains to stop them escaping. They could be bought and sold like cattle.

Slaves would have been made to wear iron chains like these.

## Quick FACTS

- Celtic society was made up of four main groups: nobles, freemen, labourers and slaves.
- Chieftains were noblemen who were warriors.
- Druids and bards were noblemen of learning.
- Women could be druidesses.
- Freemen were mostly farmers or craftsmen.
- Labourers and slaves were not free.
- Slaves did the worst jobs.

Celtic craftsmen created magnificent helmets for their chieftains, like this French one from 400 BCE.

# Make this

Some Celtic chieftains wore helmets into battle. But decorative helmets (see p. 8) were mainly worn at important events and festivals. Make your own magnificent helmet from papier-mâché and cardboard.

**1** Blow up a balloon and sit it in a bowl. Cover the top half in three layers of papier-mâché, made with torn up newspaper and watered-down PVA glue. Leave to dry overnight.

**2** Carefully remove the balloon and neatly trim the edge. This is the main part of your Celtic helmet.

Wear your helmet to become a chieftain. To see what Celtic helmets that were worn in battle look like, visit museums that have Celtic displays.

TIP: Instead of painting your helmet, try covering it with gold craft foil so it looks like it is made from real metal.

**3** Cut out two cheek flaps from cardboard. You can copy the shape shown (top right) or design your own.

**4** Paint the helmet, cheek flaps and a small polystyrene ball with gold or silver paint. Leave to dry.

**5** Attach the cheek flaps to opposite sides of the helmet with sticky tape. Glue the polystyrene ball on top.

# WAY OF LIFE

The Celts lived in small villages. War between tribes was common, so many villages were built on hills and surrounded by banks and ditches. We call these hill forts.

Maiden Castle is a large Iron Age hill fort in Dorset, England.

## Hill forts and houses

Some hill forts were lived in all year round. Other hill forts were only used during certain seasons, or if villagers were threatened with attack. The steep sides and deep ditches around a hill fort made it harder to attack. Celts lived in wooden **roundhouses** with cone-shaped roofs. The roofs

These reconstruction Iron Age roundhouses have cone-shaped, thatched roofs.

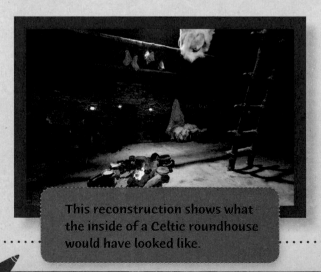

This reconstruction shows what the inside of a Celtic roundhouse would have looked like.

## War

The Celts were fearsome warriors and loved fighting. Neighbouring tribes were often at war with one another. Celtic warriors fought with iron **longswords**, spears, daggers, slings and battle-axes. Some fought naked. Celtic chieftains rode into battle in horse-drawn chariots, to the sound of war-trumpets and blood-curdling war cries.

A Celtic war trumpet is called a carnyx. The end of this one (where the sound comes out) is shaped like the head of a **wild boar**.

### HAVE A GO

There are Celtic hill forts in many parts of Britain and Europe and many stone brochs in Scotland. Ask your parents or carer if you can visit a Celtic fort or village. Use the Internet or your local library to find the site nearest to where you live.

were **thatched** with straw. The wood has long since rotted away, but we can still find the remains of holes left by posts. The holes show the shape of the building. Scottish Celts built round stone towers called **brochs**.

The remains of a Celtic broch in Scotland.

### QUIZ TIME!

The Celts invented something to help with washing. What was it?

a. **toothpaste**

b. **washing powder**

c. **soap**

Answer on page 32.

**?** **What clothing did the Celts wear? Turn the page to find out.**

## What did the Celts look like?

Many Celts had red or fair hair. The men grew long, drooping moustaches. Most Celts were tall and strong, which frightened their enemies. One Greek writer said the men: 'are terrifying to look at, with deep, rough voices. Their women are as tall as their husbands and just as strong.'

This man is wearing Celtic-style clothing.

Many Celts used a plant called woad to dye wool blue.

## Clothing

Roman writers report that Celts wore colourful clothing, made from wool that was dyed before being woven. The dye came from plants, such as woad or weld. Their clothes often had checked patterns. Men wore belted **tunics** over trousers. Women wore long tunics. In cold weather people wore cloaks. Wealthy people wore jewellery, such as bracelets, rings and open collars called **torcs** (pp. 20–21).

## Quick FACTS

- British Celts lived in roundhouses. Villages were often built on hills to help protect them from attack.
- Celtic tribes were often at war with one another.
- Celts wore woollen clothes.
- Rich people wore jewellery.

# Make this

In cold weather, Celtic people wore cloaks fastened with a brooch and pin. Make a Celtic brooch so you can dress like a Celt.

You can make all kinds of Celtic patterns with string. Find pictures in books or on the Internet to help you create different brooch designs.

**1** Draw a circle on some stiff cardboard and another circle inside it as shown. Cut out the larger circle. Cut through the larger circle so you can cut out the smaller circle inside.

**2** Glue a thin piece of string onto the brooch in a pattern like the one shown. Leave to dry.

**3** Paint the string and the rest of the brooch with gold paint. Leave to dry. (You may need more than one layer of paint.)

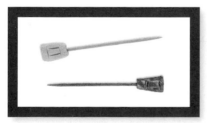

**4** For the pin, put a blob of modelling **clay** on the end of a cocktail stick. Shape and make a pattern in it as shown. When the clay has dried, paint the pin with gold paint. Leave to dry.

**5** Use a piece of checked fabric or a picnic blanket as a cloak. Carefully push the pin through the fabric to fasten your cloak. (Each end of the pin should rest on the brooch.)

**!** Make sure you ask permission if you use a blanket.

13

# FOOD AND FARMING

**The Celts grew most of their own food. They also hunted wild animals, caught fish and gathered nuts and berries. We know what they ate from remains such as grain, seeds, bones and cooking pots found at ancient sites.**

## Crop and animals

Celtic farmers reared cattle, pigs, sheep, goats, ducks and chickens. These animals provided meat, milk, wool, **hides** and eggs. The Celts also kept bees for honey. Horses and **oxen** pulled ploughs and carts. The main crops grown were wheat, barley, oats and beans. Grain was ground into flour and used to make bread, cakes and porridge.

We still eat some of the same foods that Celtic people ate during the Iron Age.

Emmer wheat

Mussels

Fava beans

Oats

Wild boar

Honey

Iron Age farmers used oxen to pull ploughs across their fields.

# Farming year

In spring, Celtic farmers ploughed their fields using teams of horses or oxen. Their light ploughs only scratched the surface, so they had to plough twice, in a criss-cross pattern. Metal **hoes** were used to root out weeds. In autumn, crops were harvested by hand, using curved blades called sickles.

An Iron Age sickle with its curved blade.

**HAVE A GO**
Compare Celtic and modern farming methods. The modern farming year is not so different – crops are still sown in spring and harvested in autumn. But some tools and methods are very different. Think about the machinery modern farmers use to plough, sow, weed and harvest crops.

**?** Were the Celts messy eaters?
Turn the page to find out.

## Feasts

Celtic chieftains held feasts to celebrate victory in battle. The Romans reported these feasts could go on for days, with many courses. There was roast meat – often wild boar – and stews bubbling in **cauldrons**. Food was washed down with ale, wine, or **mead**. Bards sang songs and recited poetry to entertain the guests.

The Celts would often serve a whole wild boar at a feast. It was their favourite meat.

## Table manners

At feasts, guests sat around a low table. They ate with their fingers, or used a knife or spoon. Bits of food would often get tangled in Celtic men's long moustaches! Feasts could get quite rowdy. The bravest warrior was given the best cut of meat, but if another warrior believed that he was the bravest, a fight would often break out.

### QUIZ TIME!
What is the drink mead made from?

a. **apples**
b. **honey**
c. **milk**

Answer on page 32.

## Quick FACTS

- Celtic farmers grew crops and kept cattle, pigs, sheep and goats.
- Farm tools included ploughs, hoes and sickles.
- Celtic chieftains held feasts to celebrate victory in battle.

# Make this

Oatcakes were a favourite Celtic food. They were made with oatmeal and flour, which was ground between two stones. The Celts ate their oatcakes plain, but you can eat them with butter, cheese, jam or honey.

## INGREDIENTS

115g oatmeal
40g flour
Pinch of salt
Pinch of bicarbonate of soda
30g melted butter
Water

To make flour, cereal grains had to be ground by hand. The Celts used stones – called quern-stones – to grind the grains. It was hard work to make a lot of flour!

**1** Put all of the dry ingredients into a bowl. (The oatmeal, flour, salt and bicarbonate of soda.)

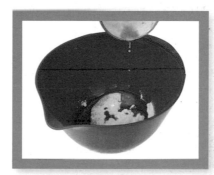

**2** Pour in the melted butter and add water a little at a time. Mix until you have a stiff dough.

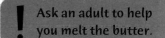 **!** Ask an adult to help you melt the butter.

**3** Tip the dough onto a floured board and roll it out until it is a few millimetres thick.

**4** Cut out circles using a cookie cutter and put them on a baking tray. Bake at 200°C for 10–15 minutes. Remove from the oven and leave to cool on a wire rack.

**!** Ask an adult to help you use the oven.

# IRON AGE CRAFTS

**The Celts were skilled in crafts such as metal-working, pottery and weaving. Many of the techniques they used are still in use today.**

## Coming of iron

Before the time of the Celts, tools and weapons were made of bronze. Celtic blacksmiths were among the first to make them from iron, by melting rock containing iron in a **furnace**. Iron was much harder and tougher than bronze. Every village would have had a blacksmith's shop.

**HAVE A GO**
Many of the Celtic iron objects that have been found are rusty and damaged. This is because there is **oxygen** in air and water, which causes the metal to rust. Look at modern metal objects that have been left outside, such as a bike. Can you see any rust on them too?

This iron axe head is decorated with a horse and rider.

This iron dagger was found in London, England. It has been damaged by rust.

# Pottery and glass

Celtic potters made clay pottery on a wheel, using techniques and technology learned from Europe. The finished pots were baked on a fire or in an oven. The Celts also made glass. Coloured glass was used to decorate objects using a technique called **enamelling**. Enamelling was used to add bright, jewel-like colours to objects.

This beautifully decorated Iron Age pot was made in Italy.

# Weaving

Every Celtic home had a **loom**, on which women and girls wove the family's clothing. Wool was spun into thread and then dyed beautiful colours. On an upright loom, weights held the vertical threads (the **warp**) in place, while the horizontal threads (the **weft**) were woven in between.

As this copy of a loom shows, Iron Age looms were made from wood. Stones were used as weights.

## QUIZ TIME!

Why were clay pots baked in an oven?

a. to keep them warm
b. to make the clay soft and bendy
c. to make the clay dry and hard

Answer on page 32.

**?** What other metals did the Celts use to make objects? Turn the page to find out.

The famous silver Gundestrup Cauldron was made by Celtic smiths around 300 BCE. It was found in Denmark but we don't know exactly where it was made.

## Jewellery

Celtic smiths worked bronze, gold and silver to make rings, torcs and bracelets. Jewellery and other objects were often decorated with swirling patterns. Craftspeople drew these patterns using compasses, which may have been a Celtic invention. Gods or animals, such as deer, dogs, wild boar and birds were also shown.

Celtic coins made of gold were decorated with swirling patterns, or animals, such as horses.

## Quick FACTS

- The Celts were among the first people to use iron.
- Jewellery and metalwork were decorated with animals or swirling patterns.
- Pottery was made on a potter's wheel.

This gold torc was found in Norfolk, England. It is one of the most beautiful Celtic objects that has ever been found.

# Make this

Metal collars called torcs were worn by Celtic men and women. Blacksmiths twisted together many thin gold or silver threads to make these open-ended collars. You can make your own torc from garden wire.

You could paint your torc silver instead of gold. Or you could make a smaller version to create a Celtic bracelet. (You will need to use a shorter length of garden wire for this.)

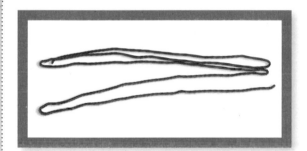

**1** Measure around your neck with a tape measure and add 3 cm. Cut a piece of garden wire five times longer than the measurement. Fold the wire into five equal sections.

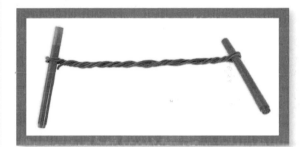

**2** Put two thick felt-tip pens into the loops at either end. Twist one of the pens until the wire starts to twist around itself as shown.

**3** Take out the pens and then put tape around the ends, in front of the loops. Make sure the tape covers both cut ends of the wire. Bend the wire into a circle.

**4** Paint your torc all over with gold acrylic paint. Leave to dry. The bendy wire will allow you to open and close the torc when you put it around your neck.

# RELIGION AND BELIEFS

**The Celts seem to have been very religious, but we don't know exactly what they believed.**

## Gods and goddesses

The Celts worshipped many gods and goddesses, but we don't know many of their names, because the Celts didn't write them down. It was the Romans who wrote down most of the Celtic gods' names we know today. We also know about Celtic religion through the carvings and statues they made of their many different gods and goddesses and through Greek and Roman writing. A Roman writer said that 'Britain is spellbound by magic.'

This drawing shows Celtic druids in a forest, worshipping their gods.

The figure on this panel of the Gundestrup Cauldron (see p. 20) is thought to be Cernunnos, the god of hunting.

# Worshipping gods

Gods and goddesses were worshipped for different reasons. For example, Sucellus was worshipped as a god of farming. The gods were often linked to places, such as rivers, waterfalls, springs and wells. Many other watery places were thought to be holy. So were oak trees and mistletoe. Celtic druids performed religious **rites** in oak forests or by water.

Waterfall

Oak tree

Mistletoe

# Festivals

Celtic festivals celebrated the seasons. The feast of Imbolc at the start of spring honoured the goddess Brigit. At Beltane on 1 May, cattle were blessed by being driven between bonfires. The autumn harvest festival, Lughnasa, honoured the god Lug. The Celts believed the spirits of the dead walked during Samhain in November.

## HAVE A GO

The customs of May Day reflect the Celtic festival of Beltane. The festival of Samhain has become Halloween and All Soul's Day. Find out more about Celtic festivals at the library or on the Internet. What similarities and differences can you find between Celtic and modern festivals?

## QUIZ TIME!

Who was the Celtic goddess of horses?

a. **Epona**
b. **Fand**
c. **Sabrina**

Answer on page 32.

**?** Did the Celts believe in life after death? Turn the page to find out.

## Burials

The Celts believed a person's spirit lived on after death. People were buried with belongings they would need in the **afterlife**. Pottery, weapons, drinking horns, jewellery and even carts and chariots have been found in Celtic graves. Some people were buried with their favourite board game!

## Sacrifices

The Celts honoured their gods by making **sacrifices**. They did this by throwing precious objects, such as shields and swords, into lakes and rivers. Priests also sacrificed animals – and occasionally even people. In 1984, the body of a Celtic man was found in a **peat** bog called Lindow Moss, near Manchester in England. He had been hit on the head, strangled and finally stabbed before being thrown into the bog. Experts believe he had been sacrificed.

Peat bog

This bronze Celtic shield was found in the River Thames. Experts think it was an offering to the gods.

## Quick FACTS

- The Celts worshipped many different gods and goddesses.
- Celtic priests sacrificed precious objects, animals and even people to honour the gods.
- The Celts believed a person's spirit lived on after death.

# Make this

Make your own shield to sacrifice to the gods. Decorate it with beautiful patterns and Celtic knots. Smiths made the swirling patterns by hammering the back of the thin metal, but you can use paint to make yours.

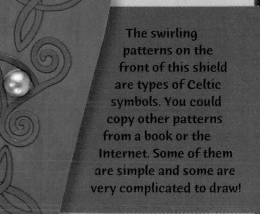

The swirling patterns on the front of this shield are types of Celtic symbols. You could copy other patterns from a book or the Internet. Some of them are simple and some are very complicated to draw!

**1** Ask an adult to cut a large rectangle from thick card. It should be about 75 cm tall, but no smaller than 50 cm.

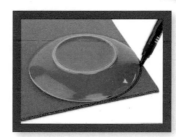

**2** Use a plate to draw a curved shape at each corner. Ask an adult to cut the corners off for you.

**3** Paint one side of the shield blue. It may need several layers of paint to cover it completely. Leave to dry.

**4** Paint half a large polystyrene ball with gold paint. Leave to dry, then glue it to the middle of the front of the shield.

Celtic knot

**5** Paint a triple spiral design and two Celtic knots as shown. Leave to dry.

A triple spiral is also called a triskele.

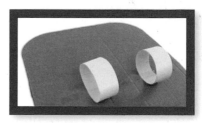

**6** Draw around the painted designs with black felt-tip pen. For the arm loops, tape two strips of thin card onto the back of the shield as shown. (The loops should be wide enough to fit your arm.)

# WHAT HAPPENED TO THE CELTS?

**The Celts ruled most of Europe for 800 years. But the Roman Empire was growing in Europe. After the Romans conquered the Celts in France, Britain was next.**

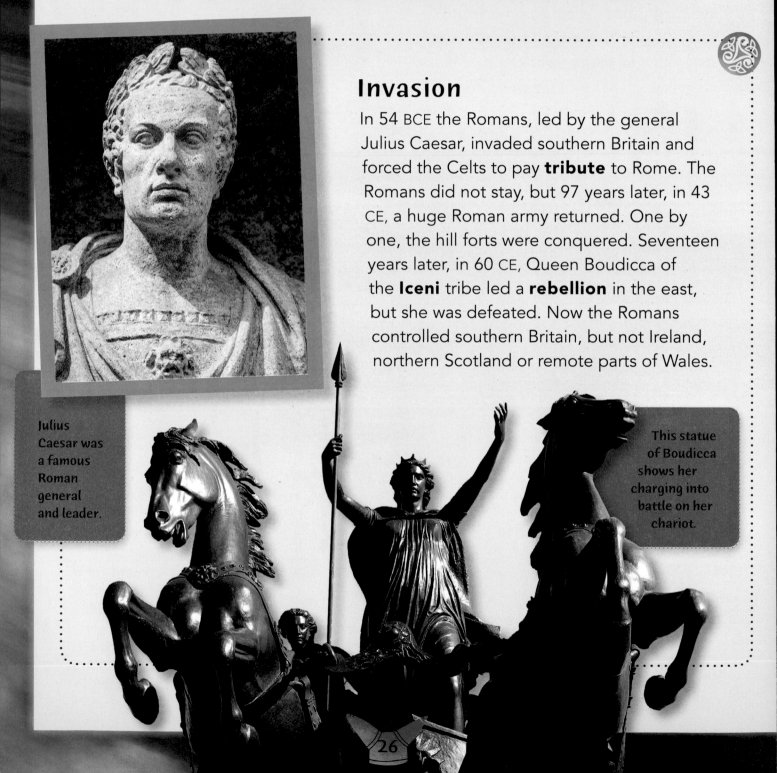

## Invasion

In 54 BCE the Romans, led by the general Julius Caesar, invaded southern Britain and forced the Celts to pay **tribute** to Rome. The Romans did not stay, but 97 years later, in 43 CE, a huge Roman army returned. One by one, the hill forts were conquered. Seventeen years later, in 60 CE, Queen Boudicca of the **Iceni** tribe led a **rebellion** in the east, but she was defeated. Now the Romans controlled southern Britain, but not Ireland, northern Scotland or remote parts of Wales.

Julius Caesar was a famous Roman general and leader.

This statue of Boudicca shows her charging into battle on her chariot.

Hadrian's Wall stretches across northern Britain. It separated Celtic Scotland from Roman-ruled Britain.

## Roman rule

In 122 CE the Roman emperor, Hadrian, ordered a wall to be built across northern Britain. It separated Celtic Scotland from the Roman south. The Romans banned the Celtic religion in Britain. Many Celts now worked for the Romans as farm labourers, servants or craftsmen. Some Celtic lords became local governors.

**QUIZ TIME!**

What name did the Romans use for the Celts?

a. **Paul**

b. **Gauls**

c. **Saul**

Answer on page 32.

## After the Romans

Roman rule for lasted 350 years. In 410 CE the Romans left Britain, but other invaders soon followed – Anglo-Saxons, Vikings and Normans. Many of the remaining Celts were pushed into Wales and Cornwall, Ireland and Scotland. Celtic culture survived in these places.

**HAVE A GO**

Celtic words survive in the names of rivers, mountains and towns all over Britain. River names such as the Thames, Tyne, Usk and Avon are Celtic. Ben and pen mean mountain. Car or caer means fort, while the endings -den and -don mean stronghold. Do places near you have Celtic names?

**?** What did the Celts leave behind? Turn the page to find out.

## What survives of the Celts?

So what is left of the Celts? Celtic languages are still spoken in Ireland, Scotland, Wales and Cornwall. Celtic words and customs survive in place names and festivals. Celtic works of art can be seen in museums and we can still visit Celtic hill forts.

This Anglo-Saxon book, which was made about 1,300 years ago, is called the Lindisfarne Gospels. It has Celtic-style art on its pages.

## Hill figures

We think the Celts carved pictures of people and animals into chalk hillsides. Similar figures can be seen today, but the original ones have been lost. The Uffington White Horse in Oxfordshire was once thought to be a Celtic hill figure. Historians now think it dates from the Late Bronze Age, around 3,000 years ago. The Celts would still have used it as religious site, because horses were such an important Celtic symbol. There is also a Celtic hill fort nearby. The Celts 'cleaned' the white chalk every few years to keep the horse in good condition.

The Uffington White Horse is a chalk hill figure.

### Quick FACTS

- The Romans had conquered southern Britain by 60 CE.
- The Romans left Britain in 410 CE, but were followed by other invaders – Anglo-Saxons, Vikings and Normans.
- Celtic language and culture survived in Ireland, Scotland, Wales and Cornwall.

# Make this

You can make your own hill figure picture by scraping away layers of wax crayon to reveal the white horse beneath.

You could use this technique to create images of other Celtic animals and plants, such as wild boar or an oak tree.

**1** Cover a sheet of card or thick A4 paper with wax, by rubbing a white candle or wax crayon all over it.

**2** Cover the layer of white wax with a thick layer of green wax crayon. You can use more than one shade of green.

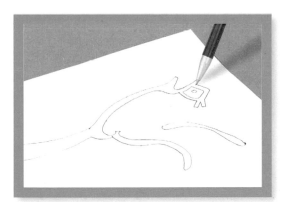

**3** Draw an outline of a horse – like the one shown – onto a thin sheet of A4 paper. Place the outline on top of the green wax and then trace over the outline with a biro. Make sure you press down quite hard.

**4** Use a blunt kitchen knife to gently scrape away the green wax inside the outline of your horse to reveal your hill figure picture.

**TIP:** You can use the green background as many times as you like. Make a new picture by colouring in your horse again with green crayon.

# GLOSSARY

**afterlife** life lived by a person's spirit after death

**ancient** from a time in the distant past

**archaeologists** experts who study objects and remains from the past

**blacksmith** a person who makes or repairs metal objects

**brochs** stone towers, built by Celts in Scotland

**bronze** metal made from copper and tin

**cauldrons** large metal cooking pots

**chieftain** a ruler of a clan, usually from a noble family

**clan** a group of Celts related to one another

**clay** type of earth that can be made into pots

**culture** art, customs and way of life of a people

**enamelling** a way of decorating metal by fusing bits of coloured glass to it

**furnace** a very hot oven where rocks with metal in them are heated up

**hides** animal skins

**hill fort** Celtic village built on a hill and surrounded by banks and ditches to protect it from attack

**hoes** long-handled tools used for weeding

**Iceni** a Celtic tribe who lived in eastern England

**Iron Age** the time after the Bronze Age, when people first used iron – a type of metal that is found in rocks

**longsword** a long sword with a cross-piece

**loom** a frame for weaving cloth

**mead** an alcoholic drink made from honey

**oxen** cattle

**oxygen** a gas in the air that living things need to breathe

**peat** plant material found in bogs that can be used as fuel

**rebellion** when people fight the government or someone in authority

**remains** things that are left over

**rent** payment to a land owner for the right to use the land

**rites** religious ceremonies

**roundhouse** a circular Celtic house with a cone-shaped roof

**sacrifice** to offer or kill something (or someone) in a religious ceremony

**thatched** a roof covered with straw or reeds

**torc** an open-ended necklace, made of twisted strands of metal

**tribe** a large group of Celts who shared a common culture. A tribe was made up of many clans

**tribute** payment made to a ruler

**tunic** a loose top that covers the body and thighs

**warp** vertical threads of weaving on a loom

**weft** horizontal threads of weaving on a loom

**wild boar** a wild pig

# BOOKS

***Britain in the Past: The Iron Age*** by Moira Butterfield (Franklin Watts 2015)
***Explore!: Stone, Bronze and Iron Ages*** by Sonya Newland (Wayland 2015)
***National Geographic Investigates: Ancient Celts*** by Jen Green (National Geographic 2008)
***The History Detective Investigates: Stone Age to Iron Age*** by Clare Hibbert (Wayland 2016)
***The Celts*** by Philip Steele (Wayland 2008)

## PLACES TO VISIT

Celtic art and objects can be seen in many museums, including these:

**British Museum, London**
**National Museum of Wales, Cardiff**
**National Museum of Scotland, Edinburgh**
**National Museum of Ireland, Archaeology and History, Dublin**

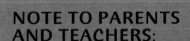

## WEBSITES

The British Museum website has information about the Celts and the Iron Age.
**www.britishmuseum.org/learning/ schools_and_teachers/resources/all_ resources/iron_age_people.aspx**

Find out more about Boudicca and Celtic life:
**http://resources.woodlands-junior.kent. sch.uk/Homework/celts.htm**

BBC Wales has Iron Age craft projects:
**www.bbc.co.uk/wales/celts/**

A BBC website with facts on the ancient peoples of Britain:
**www.bbc.co.uk/history/ancient/ british_prehistory/peoples_01.shtml**

### NOTE TO PARENTS AND TEACHERS:

Every effort has been made by the Publishers to ensure that these websites are suitable for children, that they are of the highest educational value, and that they contain no inappropriate or offensive material. However, because of the nature of the Internet, it is impossible to guarantee that the contents of these sites will not be altered. We strongly advise that Internet access is supervised by a responsible adult.

# INDEX

# QUIZ ANSWERS

**Page 5.**   **a** – The Bronze Age.

**Page 6.**   **c** – Darini. This tribe lived in what is now the northeast of Northern Ireland.

**Page 11.**   **c** – soap.

**Page 16.**   **b** – honey.

**Page 19.**   **c** – to make the clay dry and hard.

**Page 23.**   **a** – Epona. (Fand is a goddess of the sea and Sabrina is the goddess of the River Severn.)

**Page 27.**   **b** – Gauls.